HIAWATHA

HIAWATHA

Longfellow's classic poem adapted by

MICHAEL BOGDANOV

H·E·B

HEINEMANN
LONDON

Heinemann Educational Books Ltd
22 Bedford Square, London WC1B 3HH

LONDON EDINBURGH MELBOURNE AUCKLAND
HONG KONG SINGAPORE KUALA LUMPUR NEW DELHI
NAIROBI JOHANNESBURG IBADAN KINGSTON
EXETER (NH) PORT OF SPAIN

ISBN 0 435 23080 8

The performing rights in this version of HIAWATHA by
Michael Bogdanov are strictly reserved and no performance
may be given unless permission has been obtained. This
application should be made before rehearsals commence to:
Heinemann Educational Books Ltd, Drama Department,
The Windmill Press, Kingswood, Surrey

Permission will be granted only on the assumption that
the music as arranged by Jeff Teare, and used in the
National Theatre Production will be used in the production,
as it is integral to this version of the play.

The music is obtainable from Valentine Music Group Ltd.,
7 Garrick Street, Covent Garden, London WC2.

A record (or cassette) of the original National Theatre
production is available from the National Theatre Bookshop.
Issued by Multi Media Tapes MMT LP104

Cover Photograph: Laurence Burns

Typeset by The Castlefield Press of Northampton,
and printed and bound in Great Britain by
Spottiswoode Ballantyne of Colchester and London

INTRODUCTION AND NOTES ON PRODUCTION

by Michael Bogdanov

Hiawatha – Fact and Fiction

The original Hiawatha was a real person, an Indian law giver, who succeeded about the 15th century in uniting a number of tribes in a peaceful confederacy. He became confused, however, in Indian tradition, with a legendary demi-god, Son of the West Wind, whose imaginary adventures are part of the native folklore. It is of this legendary Hiawatha that Longfellow tells in his poem.

Not long before the first white men came to North America the five nations of the Iroquois organised a famous league to be called The Great Peace. The idea seems to have started with a prophet named Degandawida who had a vision of a great spruce tree with its top reaching through the sky to the land of the Master of Life. The tree was the sisterhood of all tribes and its roots were the five Iroquois tribes, an eagle perched at its top keeping watch against any enemy that might come to break the peace. It fell to a man more practical than Degandawida – Hiawatha – to set up the actual workings of the league.

In the poem, Hiawatha is a member of the Ojibwa tribe, part of the Iroquois nation. These are woodland Indians living on the shores of Lake Superior, called Gitche Gumee, meaning 'the big sea water'. These woodland Indians loved nature as if it were part of themselves, and it is their stories and legends that Henry Wadsworth Longfellow took to form the story of Hiawatha. He called Hiawatha 'the prophet of the Indian nations', who foresaw the coming of the white man and the destruction of the Indians' natural home. Chief Luther Standing Bear of the Oglala Band of Sioux said 'we did not think of the great open plains, the beautiful rolling hills and the winding streams with tangled growth as

iii

"wild"; only to the white man was nature a "wilderness" and only to him was the land "infested" with "wild animals" and "savage" people. To us it was tame, earth was bountiful and we were surrounded with the blessings of the Great Mystery. Not until the hairy man from the East came, and with brutal frenzy heaped injustices upon us and the families we loved, was it "wild" to us. When the very animals of the forest began fleeing from his approach then it was that for us the "wild west" began.'

Longfellow and the Adaptation

The American poet Henry Wadsworth Longfellow lived from 1807–1882. He was born in Portland, Maine, and became a professor of modern languages at Harvard. He took a great interest in the history and folklore of the Red Indians, particularly the tribes who inhabited the shores of the Great Lakes of North America. *The Song of Hiawatha* was his first published work.

The metre of *Hiawatha* is borrowed from a Finnish collection of poems that Longfellow had studied. The lines are all unrhymed and follow a simple rhythm of accented and unaccented syllables like the beat of a tomtom. This simple device allows the natural rhythm of the Indian culture to flow through the lines. Longfellow introduces words and names that are almost poems in themselves, which, together with his skillful use of alliteration and repetition, give the poem a dignity and serenity. It has been necessary in the adaptation for the stage to cut a large amount of the poem. Therefore only certain stories have been selected to illustrate the text; that is, those that I thought I could transfer visually and physically into epic stage imagery. In order to provide a coherent narrative to the adaptation I have changed some sequences around so that there is a logic to the development of the story. I have had on some occasions to amplify the original poem with some rather sub-standard writings of my own in order to make the links and the story clear. I make no apologies for these travesties of Longfellow's style but only plead that they are artistically necessary in order to bind the whole adaptation together.

The Production

Thorough research into the customs and traditions of the North American Indian is necessary to transfer *Hiawatha* to the stage. This research should form the background to any production for there is nothing worse than the token portrayal of another culture. There are many books available to the student and researcher in bookshops and in libraries. Those that I found most useful are listed in the Selected Bibliography. I must emphasise that it is vital there is no patronising of the characters and customs.

Starting from this background research I built up a visual identity for the production. I began with the simple use of sticks and cloths to illustrate certain visual elements. The sticks were used for forests, to build tipis, to make barriers, to be hunting staves and spears. These sticks were natural birch poles, the birch being a tree found on the shores of the Great Lakes from which the Indians made their canoes. I used blankets to be cloaks, puffs of smoke, swirling winds, snow etc, these images once begun are never ending.

Improvisation with poles can very soon create a whole new world for the poem, a little imagination transforming them into anything you wish them to be. I created a big white disc to become the moon, the sun, the stars, to provide lighting effects that illustrated nature and the outdoors. I surrounded the action with the framework of a giant tipi – the traditional North American Indian tent – to both enclose the production, and at the same time to use as a silhouette lighting effect in front of the suspended disc. I used enormous sound effects; swirling wind, cracking thunder, eerie sounds, water, anything that provided the natural outdoor feel of the Indian way of life. I devised simple rituals, based on research, for marriage, birth and death ceremonies – smoking the peace pipe, greeting, wooing, hunting, blessing etc, and most of all I instilled the production with a sense of ritual and rhythm.

Percussion plays an enormous part in this production, everything is accompanied by drums or sounds of some kind. Every step that is taken is in the form of a ritualistic movement and the dances in themselves illustrate, through the songs, the hunting of a bear, the chasing of a beaver, the celebration of a wedding or the birth of a child.

The seasons and the hours rule the play and the lighting should reflect the change of mood, through the change of seasons and the change of time. Most of all, to create spirits in the sky and the feeling of the descent from heaven and earth, I used a hand-pushed forklift truck to raise up the great Giche Manito; to lift Hiawatha in his canoe high up in front of a silhouetted sunset disc; to take Pau-Puk-Keewis up into the sky and send him plunging to the earth as a swan. It is not essential to use a forklift truck for these effects but some substitute must be found; it would be possible merely to provide a platform in front of the disc for people to climb up to and stand silhouetted. The only disadvantage to this is that it would inevitably hamper central entrances, unless a path could be found underneath the platform. This would be a matter for each individual production to solve. It does however remain a central component of the imagery of the piece.

A good percussionist is essential, somebody who can create all the sounds that inhabit the text, and somebody who can drive the rhythm of the show along. For those who have a bent for colour and design, the props and the costumes provide an enormous opportunity to explore the wonderful texture of Indian crafts — from headdresses to pipe stems, from war clubs to canoes. Most of the sequences were arrived at through mime and improvisation. Once a basic image had been found we explored the various ways it could be applied, cast members often supplying many of the solutions to what should be an exciting process of discovery. Finally, although it is possible to follow the original production from the directions given in the text, it will be up to every group of people to create their own visual images.

You must follow your own train of thought through the text and devise matching images for the poetry. Remember, that above all, the North American Indian was used to living by nature, was naturally fit and exceedingly athletic. Any production that can incorporate the physical attributes of its company is a production that is going to succeed.

The Songs and Dances

The songs and dances used in *Hiawatha* are adapted from traditional American Indian forms. The songs come from many different tribes including the Ojibwe, the Onondaga, Ottowa, Algonquin, Mohawk and Sioux, and have been 'Europeanised' to make them as accessible as possible to non-Amerindian performers and audiences. Most are in a very simple 2/4 rhythm, though at least two defy regular time and are performed as the individual chooses. The dances used are the Stomp (accented step on the on-beat, other foot dragged-to on the off); and the Pow-Wow (heel-toe used during the Wedding Chant). The lyrics to the songs are largely untranslatable as many are in fact only chants with no literal meaning at all; though there are exceptions, such as the Wedding Hymn, which is actually an Ojibwe Catholic hymn. Other music for the production has been devised using a variety of rattles, drums and wooden pipes by the company.

Notes for Amateur Productions

Throughout the text I have used certain abbreviations; these are listed below along with a selection of books and some of the main areas to explore to get the most out of your production.

Terms
L.X. – Lighting – or lighting effect
F.X. – Sound – or sound effect
D.S. – Down Stage
U.S. – Up Stage
D.C. – Down Centre

Skills
Musical instruments
Gymnastics/acrobatics
Mime
Improvisation
Drumming

Dancing
Singing
Stick fighting
Mask work
Ritual
Wrestling

Some Important Effects (or equivalents)
Fork lift truck
Giant frame of tipi
Padded floor
Mass of parachute silk
Birch canoe
Suspended white disc to light
Giant drum

Selected Bibliography

The Indian Book: Songs and Legends of the American Indians, Dover (Dover publish many books on Indian Culture)

Portraits of North American Indian Life, Edward S. Curtis, Barrie & Jenkins, 1972

North American Indian Art, Siebert and Smirnova, Paul Hamlyn, 1967

'Sacred Circles, 2000 Years of North American Indian Art', Exhibition, Hayward Gallery, Oct–Jan 1977. Introductory Material for Schools to Sacred Circles Exhibition, Arts Council of Great Britain, 1977.

Indians of the United States, Clark Wisler, Doubleday & Co, 1940

The North American Indians, Christopher Davis, Hamlyn, 1969

The American Heritage Book of Indians, Magazine of History, Eyre & Spottiswood, 1968

The Vanishing Race, selections from Edward S. Curtis's 'The North American Indians', M. Gidley, David and Charles, 1976

People of the First Man, Life Among the Plains Indians, Karl Bodmer, Clarke & Irwin Co, Toronto, 1976

Indians (Contemporary photographs of North American Indians 1847–1929), Joanna Cohan Scherer and Jean Burton Walker, Octopus Books, 1974

Pictorial History of the American Indian, Oliver Lafarge, Spring Books, 1956

Organisations
Commonwealth Institute Library, London
Canadian Embassy Library, London
American Museum, Bath
Museum of Mankind, London

THE CHARACTERS

A Company of Indians:
     Nawadaha — the Story-teller
     Gitche Manito — the Mighty
     Nokomis — Hiawatha's Grandmother
     Mudjekeewis — the West Wind
     Hiawatha
     Iagoo — the Great Boaster
     Chibiabos — the Singer
     Kwasind — the Strong Man
     Kwasind's Mother
     Kwasind's Father
     Minnehaha
     Pau-Puk-Keewis — the Dancer

Famine
Fever

A Cavalry Officer

THE FIRST NATIONAL THEATRE
PRODUCTION OF HIAWATHA

This adaptation, which opened at the Olivier Theatre on 10 December 1980, is based on the version first performed by the Young Vic Theatre Company on 29 November 1978.

The National Theatre Company

Nawadaha	James Carter
Gitche Manito	William Sleigh
Nokomis	Yvonne Bryceland
Mudjekeewis	Robert Oates
Hiawatha	Frederick Warder
Iagoo	John Normington
Chibiabos	Joss Buckley
Kwasind	Michael Fenner
Kwasind's Mother	Jane Evers
Minnehaha	Terry Diab
Pau-Puk-Keewis	Jeff Teare

The Production directed by Michael Bogdanov

Designer	Marty Flood
Music	Jeff Teare
Drums	Michael Gregory

xii

Hiawatha

THE SET: *The framework of a giant Tipi forms the entire setting. Eight struts meeting in the middle with a larger gap at the front, for sight-lines, and at the back, for entrances. The circular floor, of canvas and painted with an Indian motif, is padded to allow for physical work and acrobatics. In the background hangs a large circular white disc, which can be lit from behind to create moonlight, sunset, day etc. On either side of the set are prop-racks to hold masks, poles, clothes etc. Already pre-set, clipped or hung to poles of the Tipi and on the floor, are the main props and birch-poles that the actors will use. Each actor has a set place to which he or she will return. There is a special place for the percussionist which he will occupy throughout the performance. The lighting is dim and atmospheric.*

ACT ONE

In the distance, as the houselights go, drumming is heard, coming closer. The entire COMPANY *enter, performing a stomp dance and beating out a throbbing rhythm on hand tom-toms held under their arms. They enter single-file from the back and circle inside the Tipi. They sing three verses.*

CHORUS:
> Yo Yo Wi Ha
> Wo Da Wi Ha Hi Ya Ya

1

Yo Yo Wi Ha
Wo Da Wi Ha Hi Ya Ya
Yo Yo Wi Ha
Wo Da Wi Ha Hi Ya Ya
Yo Yo Wi Ha

Yo Yo Wi Ha
Wo Da Wi Ha Hi Ya Ya
Yo Yo Wi Ha
Wo Da Wi Ha Hi Ya Ya
Yo Yo Wi Ha
Wo Da Wi Ha Hi Ya Ya
Yo Yo Wi Ha

Yo Yo Wi Ha
Wo Da Wi Ha Hi Ya Ya
Yo Yo Wi Ha
Wo Da Wi Ha Hi Ya Ya
Yo Yo Wi Ha
Wo Da Wi Ha Hi Ya Ya
Yo Yo Wi Ha

*Freeze on final note of third verse. Move to sides to
slow beat. From back, slowly, comes* THE STORY-
TELLER. *He carries a peace-pipe wrapped in animal
skin, lays it down.* COMPANY *hum in back-ground
to description. During dialogue* THE STORY-TELLER
*produces coloured silk handkerchieves from his
costume to correspond to the images.*

ONE:
    In the Vale of Tawasentha
    In the green and silent valley,
    Dwelt the singer Nawadaha.

TWO:
    Round about the Indian village
    Spread the meadows and the corn-fields.

2

THREE:
> And beyond them stood the forest,
> Green in summer, white in winter,
> Ever sighing, ever singing.

FOUR:
> There he sang of Hiawatha,
> Sang the Song of Hiawatha,

FIVE:
> How he lived, and toiled, and suffered,
> That the tribes of men might prosper,
> That he might advance his people!

SIX:
> Ye who love the haunts of nature,
> Love the sunshine of the meadow,

SEVEN:
> Love the shadow of the forest,
> Love the wind among the branches

EIGHT:
> And the rain-shower and the snow-storm,
> And the rushing of great rivers
> Through their palisades of pine-trees,
> And the thunder of the mountains,

ONE:
> Listen to these wild traditions,
> To the Song of Hiawatha!

Drum, THE COMPANY *perform one verse of stomp*

CHORUS:
> Yo Yo Wi Ha
> Wo Da Wi Ha Hi Ya Ya
> Yo Yo Wi Ha
> Wo Da Wi Ha Hi Ya Ya
> Yo Yo Wi Ha

3

Wo Da Wi Ha Hi Ya Ya
Yo Yo Wi Ha

Lighting change. All move to positions as set. THE
STORY-TELLER *sits S.C. and unwraps pieces of
peace-pipe. From back comes* GITCHE MANITO *and
rises up in front of white disc. In the original production a small fork-lift truck was used. However, anything that will raise the level will do, e.g. a step ladder.
The image is repeated often, so some solution must
be found. The best lighting effect is to make him
float in front of the sun in a magnificent floor-length
feather head dress.*

THE PEACE PIPE

THE STORY-TELLER:
On the Mountains of the Prairie,
On the great Red Pipe-stone Quarry,
Gitche Manito, the mighty,
Stood erect, and called the nations,
Called the tribes of men together.
From the red stone of the quarry
With his hand he broke a fragment,
Moulded it into a pipe-head,
Shaped and fashioned it with figures;
From the margin of the river
Took a long reed for a pipe-stem,
With its dark green leaves upon it;
Decked it with his brightest feathers
Filled the pipe with bark of willow,
Breathed upon the neighbouring forest,
Made its great boughs chafe together,
Till in flame they burst and kindled.

TWO INDIANS *cross birch-poles and whip them
away as a* THIRD *throws out a tongue of red silk
in the air for fire. Thunder and lightning F.X.*

4

And erect upon the mountains,
Gitche Manito, the mighty,
Smoked the calumet, the Peace-Pipe,
As a signal to the nations.

INDIANS *create smoke by waving white blankets
to climax.*

And the smoke rose slowly, slowly,
Through the tranquil air of morning,
First a single line of darkness,
Then a denser, bluer vapour,
Then a snow-white cloud unfolding,
Like the tree-tops of the forest,
Ever rising, rising, rising,
Till it touched the top of heaven.

*Thunder and lightning. Blankets are whisked away.
Masks and tomahawks are taken from poles.*

From the Vale of Tawasentha,
From the far-off Rocky Mountains,
From the Northern lakes and rivers,
All the tribes beheld the signal,
Saw the distant smoke ascending,
The Pukwana of the Peace-Pipe.

War Dance

Down the rivers, o'er the prairies,
Came the warriors of the nations,

INDIANS *dive and roll over* THE STORY-TELLER
*with a war whoop as the name of their tribe is called
out.*

Came the Delawares and Mohawks,
Came the Choctaws and Comanches,
Came the Shoshonies and Blackfeet,
Came the Mandans and Dacotahs,

Came the Hurons, the Ojibways,
All the warriors drawn together.
By the signal of the Peace-Pipe.

And they stood there on the meadow,
With their weapons and their war-gear,
Painted like the leaves of autumn,
Painted like the sky of morning,
Wildly glaring at each other.

All face each other in two lines, up and down stage.

GITCHE:
O my children! my poor children!
I have given you lands to hunt in,
I have given you streams to fish in,
I have given you bear and bison,
I have given you roe and reindeer,
Filled the marshes full of wild-fowl,
Filled the rivers full of fishes;
Why then are you not contented?
Why then will you hunt each other?
I am weary of your quarrels,
Weary of your wars and bloodshed,
Therefore be at peace henceforward,
And as brothers live together.

I will send a Prophet to you,
A Deliverer of the nations,
Who shall guide you and shall teach you,
Who shall toil and suffer with you;
If you listen to his counsels,
You will multiply and prosper;
If his warnings pass unheeded,
You will fade away and perish!

Bathe now in the stream before you,
Wash the war-paint from your faces,
Wash the blood-stains from your fingers,

6

Bury your war-clubs and your weapons,
And as brothers live henceforwards!

All kneel. THE STORY-TELLER *throws out first a long line of blue silk, then red. Remove masks, place faces in stream.*

STORY-TELLER:
Then upon the ground the warriors
Threw their cloaks and shirts of deer-skin,
Threw their weapons and their war-gear,
Leaped into the rushing river,
Washed the war-paint from their faces.
Dark below them flowed the water,
Soiled and stained with streaks of crimson,
As if blood were mingled with it!

From the river came the warriors,
Clean and washed from all their war-paint;
On the banks their clubs they buried,
Buried all their war-like weapons.

All rise. Replace masks and weapons. Return and sit in circle. THE STORY-TELLER *takes peace-pipe from* GITCHE MANITO. THE TRIBES *pass round peace-pipe.*

And in silence all the warriors
Broke the red stone of the quarry,
Smoothed and formed it into Peace-Pipes,
Broke the long reeds by the river,
Decked them with their brightest feathers,
Smoked the Calumet, the Peace-Pipe.

GITCHE:
I will send a prophet to you,
A deliverer of the nations.

Return to positions. Wave blankets.

7

STORY-TELLER:
    And departed each one homeward,
    While the Master of Life, ascending,
    Through the opening of cloud-curtains,
    Through the doorways of the heaven,
    Vanished from before their faces,
    In the smoke that rolled around him,
    The Pukwana of the Peace-Pipe!

Thunder. Lightning. Blankets are thrown in air, then retreat. Flute. Lighting change. THE STORY-TELLER *comes forward with* NOKOMIS *standing on his shoulders.*

HIAWATHA'S CHILDHOOD

STORY-TELLER:
    Downward through the evening twilight,
    In the days that are forgotten,
    From the full moon fell Nokomis,
    Fell the beautiful Nokomis.

NOKOMIS *falls forward and is caught and lowered gently by the* COMPANY.

STORY-TELLER:
    Downward through the evening twilight,
    On the Muskoday, the meadow,
    On the prairie full of blossoms.
    'See, a star falls!'
    'From the sky a star is falling!'

Light on end of pole is lowered.

    There among the ferns and mosses,
    In the moonlight and the starlight,
    Fair Nokomis bore a daughter.

WENONAH *comes from back.*

8

And she called her name Wenonah,
As the first-born of her daughters.
And the daughter of Nokomis
Grew up like the prairie lilies,
Grew a tall and slender maiden,

Lift WENONAH *up on pole. Sitting.*

With the beauty of the moonlight,
With the beauty of the starlight.

And Nokomis warned her often,
Saying oft, and oft repeating,

NOKOMIS:
O, beware of Mudjekeewis,
Of the West-Wind, Mudjekeewis;
Listen not to what he tells you;
Lie not down upon the meadow,
Stoop not down upon the lilies,
Lest the West-Wind come and harm you!

Lower WENONAH. *Lies on ground.*

STORY-TELLER:
But she heeded not the warning,
Heeded not those words of wisdom,
And the West-Wind came at evening,

WEST-WIND *in large flowing white silk comes from back.*

Walking lightly o'er the prairie,
Whispering to the leaves and blossoms,
Bending low the flowers and grasses.
Found the daughter of Nokomis,
Lying there among the lilies,
Wooed her with his words of sweetness,
Wooed her with his soft caresses,
Till she bore a son in sorrow,
Bore a son of love and sorrow.

ONE:
>Thus was born my Hiawatha.

Papoos placed in arms.

TWO:
>Thus was born the child of wonder,

THREE:
>But the daughter of Nokomis,

Cover WENONAH *with black blanket. Exits.*

>Hiawatha's gentle mother,
>In her anguish died deserted
>By the West-Wind, false and faithless,
>By the heartless Mudjekeewis.

Construct tipi with seven poles leaning against each other, gap at front. Lighting change. Water. NOKOMIS *and* HIAWATHA *sit in front.*

STORY-TELLER:
>By the shores of Gitche Gumee,
>By the shining Big-Sea-Water,
>Stood the wigwam of Nokomis,
>Daughter of the Moon, Nokomis,
>Dark behind it rose the forest,
>Bright before it bent the water.
>There the wrinkled, old Nokomis
>Nursed the little Hiawatha.

OWL SONG

NOKOMIS: Ku Ku Ku Nuchi Gaden An

HIAWATHA: Ku Ku Ku Nuchi Gaden An

NOKOMIS: Ku Ku Ku Nuchi Gaden An

HIAWATHA: Ku Ku Ku Nuchi Gaden An

NOKOMIS: Nuchi Gaden An

HIAWATHA: Nuchi Gaden An

10

BOTH:　　　　Tu Da Nin Gagu On
　　　　　　　Nuchi Gaden An

　　　　　　　Ku Ku Ku Nuchi Gaden An
　　　　　　　Ku Ku Ku Nuchi Gaden An
　　　　　　　Nuchi Gaden An
　　　　　　　Tu Da Nin Gagu On
　　　　　　　Nuchi Gaden An

NOKOMIS,　　 Ku Ku Ku Nuchi Gaden An
HIAWATHA　　 Ku Ku Nuchi Gaden An
and　　　　 Nuchi Gaden An
CHORUS:　　　 Tu Da Nin Gagu On
　　　　　　　Nuchi Gaden An

　　　　　　　Ku Ku Ku Nuchi Gaden An
　　　　　　　Ku Ku Ku Nuchi Gaden An
　　　　　　　Nuchi Gaden An
　　　　　　　Tu Dan Nin Gagu On
　　　　　　　Nuchi Gaden An

IAGOO:

Many things Nokomis taught him
Of the stars that shine in heaven;

Shadow play behind disc. Effects are created by THE
STORY-TELLER *waving white silk handkerchiefs
over heads of* NOKOMIS *and* HIAWATHA.

TWO:

Showed the Death-Dance of the spirits,
Warriors with their plumes and war-clubs,

THREE:

Showed the broad, white road in heaven,
Pathway of the ghosts the shadows,

FOUR:

Saw the moon rise from the water
Saw the flecks and shadows on it.

HIAWATHA:
  What is that, Nokomis?

NOKOMIS:
  Once a warrior, very angry,
  Seized his grandmother and threw her
  Up into the sky at midnight
  Right against the moon he threw her,
  'Tis her body that you see there.

  THE STORY-TELLER *produces stream of coloured ribbons.*

STORY-TELLER:
  Saw a rainbow in the heaven.

HIAWATHA:
  What is that, Nokomis?

NOKOMIS:
  'Tis the heaven of flowers you see there.

  Owls

HIAWATHA:
  What is that? What is that, Nokomis?

NOKOMIS:
  That is but the owl and owlet
  Talking, scolding at each other.

STORY-TELLER:
  At the door on summer evenings
  Sat the little Hiawatha,
  Heard the whispering of the pine-trees

  Water. Wind.

  Heard the lapping of the water
  Saw the fire-fly, Wah-wah-taysee
  Flitting through the dusk of evening
  With the twinkle of its candle

12

Lighting up the brakes and bushes
As he sang the song of children.

Firefly dance with small lights on end of sticks whirled through the air.

FIREFLY SONG

He Yonah He Neh Yonah Heyah
He Yonah He He
Ya Hinah Nah Hoyah Nah Heyah
He Yonah He Nay Yanah Hayna Heyna
Honinah Heynah Yowah.

Lighting change

STORY-TELLER:
Then Iagoo, the great boaster,
He the marvellous story-teller,
He the traveller and the talker,
He the friend of old Nokomis,
Made a bow for Hiawatha;

Hands bow to IAGOO

From a branch of ash he made it,
From an oak-bough made the arrows,
Tipped with flint, and winged with feathers,
And the cord he made of deer-skin.

IAGOO:
Go, my son, into the forest,
Where the red-deer herd together,
Kill for us a famous roebuck,
Kill for us a deer with antlers!

Gives bow. Create forest with poles. HIAWATHA *ducks in and out.*

STORY-TELLER:
Forth into the forest straightway

13

All alone walked Hiawatha
Proudly, with his bows and arrows,
And the birds sang round him o'er him.

ONE:
'Do not shoot us, Hiawatha!'
Sang the Opechee, the robin,

TWO:
Sang the blue bird, the Owaissa,
'Do not shoot us, Hiawatha!'

THREE:
Up the oak-tree, close beside him,
Sprang the squirrel, Adjidaumo,
In and out among the branches,
'Do not shoot me, Hiawatha!'

FOUR:
And the rabbit from his pathway
Leaped aside, and at a distance
Sat erect upon his haunches,
'Do not shoot me, Hiawatha!'

STORY-TELLER:
But he heeded not, nor heard them,
For his thoughts were with the red-deer;
On their tracks his eyes were fastened,
Leading downward to the river.

Hides D.S.

Hidden in the alder bushes,
There he waited till the deer came, (*U.S.*)
Till he saw two antlers lifted,
And a deer came down the pathway,
Flecked with leafy light and shadow.

Then upon one knee uprising,
Hiawatha aimed an arrow;

ONE:
    Scarce a twig moved with his motion

TWO:
    Scarce a leaf was stirred or rustled,

STORY-TELLER:
    But the wary roebuck started,
    Stamped with all his hoofs together,
    Listened with one foot uplifted,
    Leaped as if to meet the arrow;

Shoot bow but mime arrow.
Deer somersaults over outstretched pole.

    Dead he lay there in the forest,
    Beat his timid heart no longer,
    But the heart of Hiawatha
    Throbbed and shouted and exulted,
    As he bore the red-deer homeward,
    And Iagoo and Nokomis
    Hailed his coming with applauses.

Make tipi. IAGOO *and* NOKOMIS *in front.* COM-
PANY *sit round edge.* HIAWATHA *lifts deer onto*
shoulders and stomps round circle while COMPANY
drum and sing.

DEER SONG

ALL: Man O Mandi Maja
                 Man O Mandi Maja
                 Wa Weshke Shee
                 Nee Do Dem Ha

NOKOMIS:
    From the red-deer's hide Nokomis
    Made a cloak for Hiawatha,
    Made a banquet in his honour.

15

STORY-TELLER:
All the village came and feasted.

ALL:
Man O Mandi Maja

STORY-TELLER:
And the guests praised Hiawatha

ALL:
Man O Mandi Maja

STORY-TELLER:
Called him Strong-Heart, Soan-ge-taha!

ALL:
Man O Mandi Maja

STORY-TELLER:
Called him Loon-heart, Mahn-go-taysee!

ALL:
Wa Weshke Shee
Nee Do Dem Ha

HIAWATHA *arrives front and lays deer on ground.*

HIAWATHA AND MUDJEKEEWIS

Drumroll.

STORY-TELLER:
Out of childhood into manhood
Now had grown my Hiawatha.

The COMPANY *gather downstage round* HIAWATHA.

ONE:
Swift of foot was Hiawatha:
He could shoot an arrow from him,
And run forward with such fleetness,
That the arrow fell behind him!

16

The COMPANY *forms two lines.* HIAWATHA
*shoots an arrow U.S. and off into a mattress, runs
after it, then runs back as if leading the arrow.
Arrives centre. Catches arrow thrown by* THE
STORY-TELLER. *All cheer.*

THREE:
He had mittens, Minjekahwun,
Magic mittens made of deer-skin;
When upon his hands he wore them,
He could smite the rocks asunder,
He could grind them into powder.

COMPANY *bend over to form rocks.* HIAWATHA
smashes them, karate style, with hands.

FOUR:
He had moccasins enchanted,
Magic moccasins of deer-skin;
When he bound them round his ankles,
When upon his feet he tied them,
At each stride a mile he measured!

HIAWATHA *does three handsprings.* COMPANY *run
after each one, getting progressively more tired.
Collapse at end.*

STORY-TELLER:
Much he questioned old Nokomis
Of his father Mudjekeewis;
How he became the mighty West Wind
Father of the Winds of Heaven.

HIAWATHA *and* NOKOMIS *sit left. Tipi angle is
made with a small pole leaning against one of the
main frame poles. L.X. change.*

NOKOMIS:
The Great Bear keeps the Belt of Wampum,

17

The secret belt of all the Nations,
He who has the belt around him
Is the king of all the Winds.
Becomes Kabayan the West Wind,
Your father stole the belt of Wampum
From the Great Bear of the mountains,
From the terror of the nations,
As he lay asleep and cumbrous
On the summit of the mountains.

BEAR *enters U.S. Sleeps.* MUDJEKEEWIS *creeps
slowly up on him. The actions follow the
description.*

Silently he stole upon him
Till the red nails of the monster
Almost touched him, almost scared him,
Till the hot breath of his nostrils
Warmed the hands of Mudjekeewis,
As he drew the Belt of Wampum,
Over the round ears, that heard not,
Over the small eyes, that saw not,
Over the long nose and nostrils.

Then he swung aloft his war-club,
Shouted long and loud his war-cry,
Smote the mighty Mishe-Mokwa,
In the middle of the forehead,
With the heavy blow bewildered,
Rose the Great Bear of the mountains,
But his knees beneath him trembled,
And he whimpered like a woman,
As he reeled and staggered forward,
As he sat upon his haunches.

MUDJEKEEWIS:
Hark you Bear! You are a coward,
And no Brave, as you pretended;

18

Had you conquered me in battle,
Not a groan would I have uttered;
But you, Bear! sit here and whimper,
And disgrace your tribe by crying.

BEAR *stands.*

NOKOMIS:
Then again he raised his war-club
Smote again the Mishe-Mokwa
In the middle of his forehead,
Broke his skull, as ice is broken.
Thus was slain the Mishe-Mokwa,
He the Great Bear of the mountains,
He the terror of the nations.

Whoop. Drums begin stomp rhythm. BEAR *and*
MUDJEKEEWIS *stomp round in small circles while*
COMPANY *chant.*

ALL:
Honour be to Mudjekeewis!

NOKOMIS:
Cried the Warriors, cried the old men
Henceforth he shall be the West Wind.
And hereafter and for ever
Shall he hold supreme dominion
Over all the winds of heaven.

ALL:
Call him no more Mudjekeewis,
Call him Kabayan, the West Wind!

Exit BEAR *and* MUDJEKEEWIS.

NOKOMIS:
Thus was Mudjekeewis chosen
Father of the Winds of Heaven.

STORY-TELLER:
    Then Nokomis told the secret
    Of the beauty of his mother,
    Of the falsehood of his father;
    And his heart was hot within him,
    Like a living coal his heart was.

HIAWATHA *rises. Stands centre.*

HIAWATHA:
    I will go to Mudjekeewis,
    See how fares it with my father,
    At the doorways of the West Wind,
    At the portals of the Sunset!

NOKOMIS:
    Go not forth, O Hiawatha!
    To the kingdoms of the West Wind,
    To the realms of Mudjekeewis,
    Lest he harm you with his magic,
    Lest he kill you with his cunning!

STORY-TELLER:
    But the fearless Hiawatha
    Heeded not her woman's warning.

HIAWATHA:
    Dressed for travel,

Belt and knife strapped on him.

    Armed for hunting;

Tomahawk handed.

    Forth he strode into the forest.
    For his heart was hot within him,
    Like a living coal his heart was.

COMPANY *make forest with poles.* HIAWATHA

*passes them by flinging each one in the air. They
meet to make mountain peaks.*

STORY-TELLER:
So he journeyed westward, westward,
Left the fleetest deer behind him,
Crossed the mighty Mississippi,
Passed the Mountains of the Prairie,
Came unto the Rocky Mountains,
To the kingdom of the West Wind,
Where upon the gusty summits,
Sat the ancient Mudjekeewis,
Ruler of the Winds of Heaven.

Enter MUDJEKEEWIS *on forklift. As he goes up,
a vast amount of parachute silk is pulled out from
him and rippled by the* COMPANY. *It should fill
the stage. (Any white material will do.) L.X. change.*

Filled with awe was Hiawatha
At the aspect of his father.
On the air about him wildly
Tossed and streamed his cloudy tresses.

Wind F.X.

MUDJEKEEWIS (*Voice amplified*):
Welcome, welcome, Hiawatha,
To the kingdom of the West Wind!
Long have I been waiting for you!
Youth is lovely, age is lonely.

HIAWATHA:
O Mudjekeewis,
It was you who killed my mother,
Took her young life and her beauty,
Broke the Lily of the Prairie,
Trampled it beneath your footsteps;
You confess it! you confess it!

21

STORY-TELLER:

And the mighty Mudjekeewis
Tossed his grey hairs to the west wind,
Bowed his hoary head in anguish,
With a silent nod assented.

Then up started Hiawatha,
Laid his hand upon the black rock,
His magic mittens, Minjekahwun,
Rent the jutting crag asunder,
Smote and crushed it into fragments,
Hurled them madly at his father.

Thunder/lightning. HIAWATHA *rips two black blankets off the backs of two of the company and, retaining hold of them, hurls them continuously at* MUDJEKEEWIS *throughout the sequence.*

But the ruler of the West Wind
Blew the fragments backwards from him,

Thunder/lightning

Then began the deadly conflict
Hand to hand among the mountains

Thunder/lightning

Till the earth shook with the tumult
And confusion of the battle.

Thunder/lightning

And the air was full of shoutings
And the thunder of the mountains.

Thunder/lightning

Back retreated Mudjekeewis,
Still pursued by Hiawatha
To the doorways of the West Wind,

To the portals of the Sunset.
To the earth's remotest border.

Thunder/lightning

MUDJEKEEWIS:
Hold! Hold, my son, my Hiawatha!
'Tis impossible to kill me,
For you cannot kill the immortal.
I have put you to this trial,
But to know and prove your courage;
Now receive the prize of valour!

Go back to your home and people,
Live among them, toil among them,
Cleanse the earth from all that harms it,
Clear the fishing grounds and rivers,
Slay all monsters and magicians,
All the giants, the Wendigoes,
All the serpents, the Kenabeeks,
As I slew the Mishe-Mokwa,
Slew the Great Bear of the mountains.

And at last when Death draws near you,
I will share my kingdom with you,
Ruler shall you be thenceforward!
Of the North West Wind, Keewaydin.

Exit MUDJEKEEWIS, *pulling in silk to him. Flute.*
COMPANY *form forest. L.X. change.*

STORY-TELLER:
Homeward now went Hiawatha,
Only once he paused or halted
In the Land of the Dacotahs
Saw the Arrowmaker's daughter
Minnehaha, Laughing Water,

Passes MINNEHAHA *on journey. Lifts pole up for
her to duck under.*

23

Saw the moonlight and the starlight,
In the lovely Laughing Water.

And onward now went Hiawatha,
Pleasant was the landscape round him,
Pleasant was the air above him,
For the bitterness of anger
Had departed wholly from him.

Thus was fought that famous battle
In the long days since departed,
In the kingdom of the West Wind.
But the face of Laughing Water
Would stay with him through the days.

Arrives D.F. with STORY-TELLER.

HIAWATHA'S FRIENDS

Drumroll

NOKOMIS (*Centre*):
 Two good friends had Hiawatha,

They introduce themselves.

CHIBIABOS:
 Chibiabos, the musician,

KWASIND:
 And the very strong man, Kwasind.

STORY-TELLER:
 Most beloved by Hiawatha
 Was the gentle Chibiabos,

CHIBIABOS:
 He the best of all musicians.
 He the sweetest of all singers.

ONE:
 When he sang, the village listened;

24

TWO:
　　All the warriors gathered round him,

THREE:
　　All the women came to hear him.

All sit in circle. CHIBIABOS *in middle. Night and
fire L.X.*

CHIBIABOS' SONG

CHIBIABOS:　Og I Wab Man
　　　　　　Wi Ne Mush E Nan A Weh
　　　　　　Be Mo Se Ni Si O Weh
　　　　　　Be Mo Se Ni Sweh

　　　　　　Og I Wab Man
　　　　　　Wi Ne Mush E Nan A Weh
　　　　　　Be Mo Se Ni Si O Weh
　　　　　　Be Mo Se Ni Sweh

ALL:　　　　Og I Wab Man
　　　　　　Wi Ne Mush E Nan A Weh
　　　　　　Be Mo Se Ni Si O Weh
　　　　　　Be Mo Se Ni Sweh

All whoop, followed by drumroll.

STORY-TELLER:
　　Dear, too, unto Hiawatha,
　　Was the very strong man, Kwasind,

KWASIND:
　　He the strongest of all mortals,
　　He the mightiest among many;

Drumroll.

ONE:
　　Idle in his youth was Kwasind,

TWO:
Very listless, dull, and dreamy,

THREE:
Never played with other children,

FOUR:
Never fished and never hunted.

MOTHER *and* FATHER *hold net*. TWO OF COMPANY *form tipi frame behind.*

MOTHER:
Lazy Kwasind.

STORY-TELLER:
Said his mother.

MOTHER:
In my work you never help me.
In the coldest days of winter
I must check the ice for fishing.
With my nets you never help me
Go and dry them in the sunshine.

STORY-TELLER:
Slowly from the ashes, Kwasind
Rose but made not angry answer;
Took the nets that hung together,
Dripping, freezing at the doorway.
Like a whip of straw he wrung them
Like a whip of straw he broke them.

Gets hopelessly tangled up. Rips it apart.

KWASIND:
Sorry Mum.

MOTHER:
Lazy Kwasind!

26

FATHER:
    Lazy Kwasind!

STORY-TELLER:
    Said his father.

FATHER:
    In the hunt you never help me
    Every bow you touch is broken
    Snapped asunder every arrow!
    Take this bow into the forest
    Kill for us a deer to feast on.

STORY-TELLER:
    Slowly Kwasind took the bow
    Aimed an arrow straight and true
    He the mightiest of mortals.
    He the strongest of all men.

Bow snaps. Hands arrow back. Arrow snaps.

KWASIND:
    Sorry Dad.

FATHER:
    Lazy Kwasind!

CHILDREN:
    Lazy Kwasind!
    Come and wrestle with the others.

Wrestling sequence. KWASIND *throws* COMPANY
around. This should be both spectacular and comic.

STORY-TELLER:
    In the stream he saw a beaver,
    Saw Ahmeek, the King of Beavers,
    Struggling with the rushing currents,
    Rising, sinking in the water.

*Form stream by holding poles crossways and un-
dulating up and down.*

27

Without speaking, without pausing,
Kwasind leaped into the river,
Plunged beneath the bubbling surface,
Through the whirlpools chased the beaver,
Following him among the islands,
Stayed so long beneath the water,
That his terrified companions
Cried,

CHILDREN:
Alas! Goodbye to Kwasind!
We shall never more see Kwasind!

STORY-TELLER:
But he reappeared triumphant,
And upon his shining shoulders

Lifts beaver up on shoulders in middle of poles.

Brought the beaver, dead and dripping,
Brought the King of all the beavers.

Poles make tipi. COMPANY *sit in circle round it.*
KWASIND *stomps round with beaver on shoulders.*

BEAVER SONG

CHIBIABOS:	He Ho Ya Win
ALL:	Ga Ni No Ha Wa Han
CHIBIABOS:	He Ho Ya Win
ALL:	Ga Ni No Ha Wa Han
CHIBIABOS:	He Ho Ya Win
ALL:	Ga Ni No Ha Wa Han
CHIBIABOS:	He Ho Ya Win
ALL:	Ga Ni No Ha Wa Han
CHIBIABOS:	He Ho Ya Win

ALL:	Ga Ni No Ha Wa Han
CHIBIABOS:	He Ho Ya Win
ALL:	Ga Ni No Ha Wa Han
CHIBIABOS:	He Ho Ya Win
ALL:	Ga Ni No Ha Wa Han
CHIBIABOS:	He Ho Ya Win
ALL:	Ga Ni No Ha Wa Han Ay Ya Ho

Drops beaver. Holds beaver head aloft in triumph.

STORY-TELLER:
Sing O song of Hiawatha
How he hunted, how he fished,
How he built a birch canoe.

This sequence must be worked as is practical. The idea is literally to strip a piece of bark whole from a trunk and, with some lengths of bamboo and some leather thongs, make a canoe. THE STORY-TELLER *sits D.F. and makes a tiny model of the canoe at the same time.*

HIAWATHA:
Give me of your bark, O Birch-Tree!
I a light canoe will build me,
That shall float upon the river,
Like a yellow leaf in Autumn,
Like a yellow water-lily!

The main trunk should remain upright and HIA-
WATHA *makes canoe in front of it.*

STORY-TELLER:
With his knife the tree he girdled;
Down the trunk, from top to bottom,

Sheer he cleft the bark asunder,
Stripped it from the trunk unbroken.

HIAWATHA:
Give me of your boughs, O Cedar!
My canoe to make more steady,
Make more strong and firm beneath me!

STORY-TELLER:
Through the summit of the Cedar
Went a sound, a cry of horror,
But it whispered, bending downward,

ONE:
Take my boughs, O Hiawatha!

STORY-TELLER:
Down he hewed the boughs of cedar,
Shaped them straightway to a framework,
Like two bows he formed and shaped them,
Like two bended bows together.

HIAWATHA:
Give me of your roots, O Tamarack!
My canoe to bind together,
That the water may not enter.

STORY-TELLER:
From the earth he tore the fibres,
Closely sewed the bark together,
Bound it closely to the framework.

HIAWATHA:
Give me of your balm, O Fir Tree!
So to close the seams together.

STORY-TELLER:
And he took the tears of balsam,
Smeared therewith each seam and fissure,
Made each crevice safe from water.

HIAWATHA:

Give me of your quills, O Hedgehog!
All your quills, O Kagh, the Hedgehog!
I will make a necklace of them.

STORY-TELLER:

From the hollow tree the Hedgehog
With his sleepy eyes looked at him,
Shot his shining quills like arrows,
Saying, with a drowsy murmur,
Through the tangle of his whiskers,

HEDGEHOG:

Take my quills, O Hiawatha!

STORY-TELLER:

From the ground the quills he gathered,
All the little shining arrows,
Stained them red and blue and yellow
With the juice of roots and berries;
Into his canoe he wrought them,
Round its waist a shining girdle,
Round its bows a gleaming necklace,
On its breast two stars resplendent.

*Indian sign language is painted on the upright trunk
to depict the images that follow. Flute.*

ONE:

Thus the Birch Canoe was builded

TWO:

In the valley by the river,

THREE:

In the shadow of the forest;

FOUR:

And the forest's life was in it,

31

FIVE:
All its mystery and its magic,

SIX:
All the lightness of the birch-tree,

SEVEN:
All the toughness of the cedar,

EIGHT:
All the larch's supple sinews.

HIAWATHA *kneels at head of canoe.*

CANOE SONG

HIAWATHA: Gu Yo Wan
Ne Ho Ne Ho
Gu Yo Wan A Nee E Ho
Gu Yo Wan A Ne Ho

STORY-TELLER:
And it floated on the river
Like a yellow leaf in Autumn,
Like a yellow water lily.

STORY-TELLER *slowly places tiny model in front of him. Drums.*

Forth upon the Gitche Gumee,
On the shining Big-Sea-Water,
With his fishing line of cedar,
Forth went Hiawatha.

COMPANY *lift* HIAWATHA *in canoe on to their shoulders. Move round with him.*

FISHING SONG

ALL: Gaya Wi Ho

Ya Wi Ha
Gaya Wi Ho
Ya Wi Ha
Gaya Wi Ho
Ya Wi Ha
Gaya Wi Ho Ya
Gaya Wi Ho Ya

Gaya Wi Ho
Ya Wi Ha
Gaya Wi Ho
Ya Wi Ho
Gaya Wi Ho
Ya Wi Ha
Gaya Wi Ho Ya
Gaya Wi Ho Ya

L.X. change

STORY-TELLER:
Forth to catch the sturgeon Nahma.
Taller than a tree was Nahma,
Wider than a forest glade
And his mouth a gaping cavern
Thirty feet across it measured,
Black and deep a gaping cave.

ONE:
Mishe Nahma, King of Fishes.

TWO:
All alone went Hiawatha.

HIAWATHA *stops centre, held in canoe. Wave black blankets. Dim lighting.*

STORY-TELLER:
Quiet lay the sturgeon Nahma,
Fanning slowly in the water,
Looking up at Hiawatha.

33

HIAWATHA:
Take my bait, O Sturgeon Nahma,
Come up from below the water,
Let us see which is the stronger.

STORY-TELLER:
From the white sand of the bottom
Up he rose with angry gesture,

Forklift truck rises with MEMBER OF COMPANY
in sturgeon mask and huge fins.

Quivering in each nerve and fibre,
Clashing all his plates of armour,
Gleaming bright with all his war paint;
In his wrath he darted upward,
Flashing leaped into the sunshine,
Opened his great jaws and swallowed,
Both canoe and Hiawatha!

Thunder/lightning. HIAWATHA *lowered. Dark.*

STORY-TELLER:
Down into that darksome cavern
Plunged the headlong Hiawatha,

Strange sounds.

Groped about in helpless wonder,
Till he felt a great heart beating,
Throbbing in that other darkness

Disc pulses dull red. Drums illustrate the text.

And he smote it in his anger,
With his fists, the heart of Nahma,
Felt the mighty King of Fishes,
Shudder through each nerve and fibre,
Gasp and quiver in the water,
Then was dead the King of Fishes.

34

Pulse dies. Seagull F.X.

> Then he heard a clang and flapping,
> As of many wings assembling,

SEAGULLS *in masks and white blankets move round.*
HIAWATHA *is hemmed in by poles.*

> Heard a screaming and confusion,
> As of birds of prey contending
> Saw a gleam of light above him,
> Shining through the ribs of Nahma,
> Saw the glittering eyes of seagulls,
> Gazing at him through the opening,
> Heard them saying to each other,

GULLS:
> 'Tis our brother, Hiawatha.

HIAWATHA:
> O ye seagulls, O my brothers.
> I have slain the sturgeon Nahma;
> Make the rifts a little larger,
> With your claws the opening widen
> Set me free from this dark prison.

STORY-TELLER:
> And the wild and clamorous seagulls
> Toiled with beak and claws together,

SEAGULLS *lift poles. Lights gradually build.*

> Made the rifts and openings wider
> In the mighty ribs of Nahma,
> And from peril and from prison,
> From the body of the sturgeon,
> Was released my Hiawatha.

HIAWATHA *dives out of canoe which is then taken out.*

35

NOKOMIS:
> Three whole days and nights alternate
> Old Nokomis and the seagulls
> Stripped the oily flesh of Nahma.

Poles lie on ground with sturgeon mask placed in middle.

STORY-TELLER:
> Till the waves washed through rib bones,
> Till the seagulls came no longer,
> And upon the sands lay nothing
> But the skeleton of Nahma.

SEAGULLS *retreat. Flute.*

HIAWATHA'S WOOING

STORY-TELLER:
> In the land of the Dacotahs
> Where the falls of Minnehaha
> Flash and gleam among the oak-trees,
> Laugh and leap into the valley.

ARROWMAKER *and* MINNEHAHA *sit U.S. Two make tipi frame.*

ARROWMAKER:
> There the ancient Arrowmaker
> Made his arrow-heads of sandstone,

MINNEHAHA:
> With him dwelt his dark-eyed daughter
> Wayward as the Minnehaha,
> With her moods of shade and sunshine,

STORY-TELLER:
> And he named her from the river,
> From the waterfall he named her,
> Minnehaha, Laughing Water.

HIAWATHA:

    Hiawatha's heart was full of longing
    For the lovely Laughing Water
    In the land of the Dacotahs.

HIAWATHA *sits D.S. with* NOKOMIS *in front of second tipi frame.*

NOKOMIS:

    Wed a maiden of your people
    Go not eastward, go not westward,
    For a stranger, whom we know not!

HIAWATHA:

    In the land of the Dacotahs
    Lives the Arrowmaker's daughter,
    Minnehaha, Laughing Water,
    Handsomest of all the women.
    I will bring her to your wigwam
    She shall run upon your errands
    Be your starlight, moonlight, firelight,
    Be the sunlight of my people!

NOKOMIS:

    Very fierce are the Dacotahs
    Often there is war between us
    There are feuds, yet unforgotten
    Wounds that ache and still may open.

HIAWATHA:

    For that reason if no other
    Would I wed the fair Dacotah
    That our tribes might be united
    And old wounds be healed for ever.

STORY-TELLER:

    Thus departed Hiawatha
    To the land of the Dacotahs
    To the land of handsome women.

HIAWATHA dives and leaps over poles. THE STORY-
TELLER *hands him deer's head.*

On he journeyed through the forest
Bearing with him gifts and presents
Shot a handsome roe-buck deer,
Brought it to the Arrowmaker
At the feet of Minnehaha.

All sitting U.S.

HIAWATHA:
After many years of warfare
There is peace between the Ojibways
And the tribe of the Dacotahs
That this peace may last for ever
And our hearts be more united
Give me as my wife this maiden
Minnehaha, Laughing Water
Loveliest of Dacotah women.

ARROWMAKER:
Yes, if Minnehaha wishes
Let your heart speak, Minnehaha.

STORY-TELLER:
And the lovely Laughing Water
Gave her hand to Hiawatha.

They rise.

MINNEHAHA:
I will follow you my husband.

STORY-TELLER:
From the wigwam he departed
Leading with him Laughing Water

Move D.S.

Hand in hand they went together

38

Through the woodland and the meadow
Left the Old Man standing lonely.

ARROWMAKER:
Thus it is our daughters leave us.

Flute.

STORY-TELLER:
Thus it was they journeyed homeward
Over meadow, over mountain,
Over river, hill and hollow,
Over wide and rushing rivers,
In his arms he bore the maiden.

Arrive D.S., HIAWATHA *lifts her up.*

And the sun looked down upon them saying

SUN:
Love is sunshine, hate is shadow,
Rule by love, O Hiawatha!

L.X. change.

STORY-TELLER:
From the sky the moon looked at them.

MOON:
Day is restless, night is quiet,
Rule by patience, Laughing Water.

COMPANY *makes tipi.* NOKOMIS *stands in front.*
Takes the hands of HIAWATHA *and* MINNEHAHA.

STORY-TELLER:
Thus it was that Hiawatha
To the lodge of Old Nokomis
Brought the moonlight, starlight, firelight
Brought the sunshine of his people
Minnehaha, Laughing Water.

All stomp round and out, the song gradually fading into distance.

SONG

ALL: Yo Yo Wi Ha etc.

END OF ACT ONE

ACT TWO

A very large drum is placed in the centre of the stage. The lights dim. THE COMPANY *enter one by one, in head-dresses, and sit round building up a stomp rhythm of cross-patterns. The thunderous drumming builds to a climax and then cuts off.* DRUMMER *starts stomping rhythm.* COMPANY *dress in furs etc. Hold rattles.* THE STORY-TELLER *stomps and sings.* HIAWATHA *and* MINNEHAHA *sit left and right of big drum, facing across at each other.*

DRUM DANCE

STORY-TELLER:
Sumptuous was the feast Nokomis
Made at Hiawatha's wedding.
And the wedding-guests assembled,
Clad in all their richest raiment,
Robes of fur and belts of wampum,
Splendid with their paints and plumage,
Beautiful with beads and tassels.

WEDDING CHANT

STORY-TELLER:	Hi Ya Ho
ALL:	Haya
STORY-TELLER:	Hi Ya Ho
ALL:	Haya
STORY-TELLER:	Hi Ya Ho
ALL:	Haya etc.

Drums. If possible, THE STORY-TELLER *juggles with tomahawks, somebody twirls a rope etc. Any skill to celebrate the wedding.*

IAGOO:
>Then Iagoo, the great boaster
>Saw the wedding guests assembled
>Longed to hear his pleasant stories
>His immeasurable falsehoods.

IAGOO *mimes the following sequence.*

STORY-TELLER:
>Would you listen to his boasting

TWO:
>No-one ever shot an arrow
>Half so far and high as he had,

THREE:
>Ever caught so many fishes

FOUR:
>Ever killed so many reindeer

FIVE:
>None could run so fast as he could

SIX:
>None could dive so deep as he could.

IAGOO:
>As this wonderful Iagoo.

All groan.

NOKOMIS:
>O Pau-Puk-Keewis,
>Dance for us your merry dances,
>Dance the Beggar's Dance to please us,
>That the feast may be more joyous,

That the time may pass more gaily,
And our guests be more contented!

STORY-TELLER:
Then the handsome Pau-Puk-Keewis
He the merry mischief-maker,
Whom the people call the Storm-Fool,
Rose among the guests assembled.

PAU-PUK-KEEWIS *comes centre to slow stomp rhythm.* THE STORY-TELLER *throws four hoops over his head so that they spin and bounce back into his hands.*

First he danced a solemn measure,
Very slow in step and gesture,
In and out among the pine-trees,
Through the shadows and the sunshine,
Treading softly like a panther;
Then more swiftly and still swifter,
Whirling, spinning round in circles,
Leaping o'er the guests assembled,
Eddying round and round the wigwam,
Till the leaves went whirling with him,
Till the dust and wind together
Swept in eddies round about him.

HOOP DANCE

This must be worked out with the hoops and the individual's ability to make patterns with them. It is called a 'show-off' dance.

STORY-TELLER:
Then they said to Chibiabos,
To the friend of Hiawatha,
To the sweetest of all singers,
To the best of all musicians,

MINNEHAHA:
Sing to us, O Chibiabos,

HIAWATHA:
Songs of love and songs of longing,

MINNEHAHA:
That the feast may be more joyous,

HIAWATHA:
And the time may pass more gaily,

MINNEHAHA:
And our guests be more contented!

STORY-TELLER:
And the gentle Chibiabos
Looking at fair Laughing Water
Sang he softly, sang in this wise:

CHIBIABOS *sits in middle. Lights dim.*

WEDDING HYMN

CHIBIABOS: Mari Abis Kon
Ne Ta Ba Ta A Di Jig
Wa A Se I Ne Mo Ga Le Ga A Le Ee
Te Bi Ka Di Mo Si Dig

Mari Abis Kon
Ne Ta Ba Ta A Di Jig
Wa A Se I Ne No Ga Le Ga A Le Ee
Te Bi Ka Di Mo Si Dig

ALL: Mari Abis Kon
Ne Ta Ba Ta A Di Jig
Wa A Se I Ne Mo Ga Le Ga A Le Ee
Te Bi Ka Di Mo Si Dig

Hum. Drum is taken off.

44

NOKOMIS:
> Such was Hiawatha's wedding,

IAGOO:
> Such the stories of Iagoo

PAU-PUK-KEEWIS:
> Such the dance of Pau-Puk-Keewis.

CHIBIABOS:
> Such the songs of Chibiabos.

STORY-TELLER:
> Thus the wedding-banquet ended,
> And the wedding guests departed,
> Leaving Hiawatha happy
> With the night and Minnehaha.

*All leave, humming softly. Night. In the following
sequence, long strips of green and yellow ribbon are
drawn outwards from the centre and held aloft.*
MINNEHAHA *is dressed in a black cloak and moves
round under the ribbons to stand centre. As the
lights grow brighter, the company walk round her,
gradually binding her in the green and yellow ribbon
to create the image of maize. The humming con-
tinues throughout.*

STORY-TELLER:
> All around the happy village
> Stood the maize fields, green and shining
> Filling all the land with plenty.

ONE:
> 'Twas the women who in Spring-time
> Planted the broad fields and fruitful.

TWO:
> 'Twas the women who in Autumn
> Stripped the yellow husks of harvest.

STORY-TELLER:
    To his wife, said Hiawatha,
    To his wife, the Laughing Water.

HIAWATHA:
    You shall bless tonight the corn fields
    And with the passing of your footsteps
    Draw a magic circle round them
    To protect them from destruction.

STORY-TELLER:
    When the noiseless night descended
    Broad and dark o'er field and forest
    From her bed rose Laughing Water
    Laid aside her garments wholly
    And with darkness clothed and guarded
    Covered by her tresses only
    Walked securely round the corn-fields
    Drew the sacred magic circle
    Of her footprints round the corn-fields.

*Song — 'Mari Abis Kon' — broadens behind
description.*

    And the maize field grew and ripened
    Till it stood in all its splendour
    Of its garments green and yellow.

ALL:
    Te Bi Ka Di Mo Si Dig

MINNEHAHA *throws off ribbons. Drum Roll. L.X.
change.* PAU-PUK-KEEWIS *stands in angle of main
tipi, left.* COMPANY *sit in semi-circle centre around*
IAGOO. THE STORY-TELLER *holds pole behind for
tent entrance.*

46

PAU-PUK-KEEWIS

PAU-PUK-KEEWIS:
> On the shores of Gitche Gumee
> By the shining Big-Sea-Water
> Stood the lodge of Pau-Puk-Keewis.

STORY-TELLER:
> It was he so merrily and madly
> Danced at Hiawatha's wedding.

PAU-PUK-KEEWIS:
> Now in search of new adventures,
> From his lodge went Pau-Puk-Keewis
> Came with speed into the village.

He circles the set.

ONE:
> Found the young men all assembled
> In the lodge of old Iagoo,

IAGOO:
> Listening to his monstrous stories,
> To his wonderful adventures.

All laugh. **PAU-PUK-KEEWIS** *enters under* **THE STORY-TELLER'S** *pole. Stands behind them.*

PAU-PUK-KEEWIS:
> Hark you!
> I am tired of all this talking
> Tired of old Iagoo's stories,
> Tired of Hiawatha's wisdom.
> Here is something to amuse you,
> Better than this endless talking.

Kneels D.S. in front of them. The actions follow the description.

47

STORY-TELLER:

Then from out his pouch of wolf-skin
Forth he drew, with solemn manner,
All the game of Bowl and Counters,
Pugasaing, with thirteen pieces,
White on one side were they painted.
Fourteen curious eyes stared at him,
Full of eagerness stared at him.

IAGOO:

Many games,
Many games of skill and hazard
Have I seen in different nations,
Have I played in different countries.
He who plays with old Iagoo
Must have very nimble fingers;
Though you think yourself so skilful,
I can beat you, Pau-Puk-Keewis,
I can even give you lessons
In your game of Bowl and Counters!

STORY-TELLER:

So they sat and played together,
All the old men and the young men,
Played till midnight, played till morning.
Till the cunning Pau-Puk-Keewis
Of their treasures had despoiled them,
Of the best of all their treasures.

*The game has been played on a big deer-skin. They
now divest themselves of cloaks etc and throw them
into the middle.*

ONE:

Robes of ermine,

TWO:

Robes of deer-skin,

48

THREE:
Belts of wampum,

FOUR:
Crests of feathers,

FIVE:
Warlike weapons,

SIX:
Pipes and pouches.

STORY-TELLER:
Twenty eyes glared wildly at him,
Like the eyes of wolves glared at him.

PAU-PUK-KEEWIS:
In my wigwam I am lonely,
In my wanderings and adventures
I have need of a companion,
I will venture all these winnings,
On a single throw will venture
All against the young man yonder!

YOUTH:
'Twas the youth of sixteen summers,
'Twas a nephew of Iagoo;
Face-in-a-Mist the people called him.

STORY-TELLER:
As the fire burns in a pipe-head
Dusky red beneath the ashes,
So beneath his shaggy eyebrows
Glowed the eyes of old Iagoo

IAGOO:
Ugh!

STORY-TELLER:
Seized the wooden bowl the old man,
Closely in his bony fingers

49

Shook it fiercely and with fury,
Made the pieces ring together
As he threw them down before him.
Only five pieces counted!

Then the smiling Pau-Puk-Keewis
Shook the bowl and threw the pieces;
Lightly in the air he tossed them,
And they fell about him scattered:
'Five tens! Fifty mine the game is!'

Fourteen eyes glared at him fiercely,
Like the eyes of wolves glared at him,
As he turned and left the wigwam,

YOUTH *picks up winnings, drops them in deer-skin.*
Exit under THE STORY-TELLER'S *pole.*

Followed by his Meshinauwa,
By the nephew of Iagoo,
Bearing in his arms the winnings,
Shirts of deer-skin, robes of ermine,
Belts of wampum, pipes, and weapons.

Circle set. COMPANY *construct tipi and wrap black*
blankets round it, leaving entrance front open. L.X.
change. Dawn.

Hot and red with smoke and gambling
Were the eyes of Pau-Puk-Keewis
As he wandered through the village,
In the early grey of morning,
Till he reached the farthest wigwam,
Reached the lodge of Hiawatha.

Silent was it and deserted;
No-one met him at the doorway,
No-one came to bid him welcome.

Raven's head is lifted on pole above tipi.

And aloft upon the ridge pole
Kahgahgee, the King of Ravens,
Sat with fiery eyes, and, screaming,
Flapped his wings at Pau-Puk-Keewis.

PAU-PUK-KEEWIS:
All are gone, the lodge is empty!

STORY-TELLER:
Thus it was spake Pau-Puk-Keewis
In his heart resolving mischief.

PAU-PUK-KEEWIS:
Gone is wary Hiawatha,
Gone the silly Laughing Water,
Gone Nokomis, the old woman,
And the lodge is left unguarded!

Raven's head lowered.

STORY-TELLER:
By the neck he seized the raven,
Whirled it round him like a rattle,
Like a medicine-pouch he shook it,
Strangled Kahgahgee, the raven,
From the ridge-pole of the wigwam
Left its lifeless body hanging

Throws it on top of tipi.

PAU-PUK-KEEWIS:
As an insult to its master,
As a taunt to Hiawatha.

STORY-TELLER:
With a stealthy step he entered,
Round the lodge in wild disorder
Threw the household things about him

Tears off blankets.

PAU-PUK-KEEWIS:
>As an insult to Nokomis
>As a taunt to Minnehaha.

Collapses tipi.

STORY-TELLER:
>Then departed Pau-Puk-Keewis,
>Whistling, singing through the forest.

PAU-PUK-KEEWIS' SONG

PAU-PUK-KEEWIS: Ku ku ku ku ningo sa etc.

Exit U.S.

THE HUNTING OF PAU-PUK-KEEWIS

HIAWATHA *enters from U.S.* COMPANY *start to pick up poles and blankets.*

HIAWATHA:
>Full of wrath was Hiawatha
>When he came into the village

STORY-TELLER:
>Found the people in confusion,

ONE:
>Heard of all the misdemeanours,

TWO:
>All the malice and the mischief
>Of the cunning Pau-Puk-Keewis.

HIAWATHA:
>I will slay this Pau-Puk-Keewis,
>Slay this mischief-maker!
>Not so long and wide the world is,
>Not so rude and rough the way is,

52

That my wrath shall not attain him,
That my vengeance shall not reach him!

Drums.

STORY-TELLER:
Then in swift pursuit departed
Hiawatha and the Hunters
On the trail of Pau-Puk-Keewis.

L.X. flashing lights.

CHASE SEQUENCE AND KILLING RITUAL

COMPANY *create obstacles with poles and blankets.*
HIAWATHA *chases* PAU-PUK-KEEWIS *in and out,
diving etc. Drums and noise.*

PAU-PUK-KEEWIS:
But the cunning Pau-Puk-Keewis,
Changed himself into a beaver,
Ahmeek, the great king of Beavers,

STORY-TELLER:
By a dam within the forest
Hid within the house of branches

COMPANY *make stick house.* PAU-PUK-KEEWIS
with beaver's head hides in it.

But the hunters came upon him,
Smashed his beaver house to pieces,
With their clubs to death they beat him

COMPANY *smash the stick house to pieces with
poles. They hang* PAU-PUK-KEEWIS *upside down by
his legs and process round stage with him.*

Lifted him onto their shoulders,
On their poles they homeward bore him.

HUNTING SONG

ALL:

       Man O Mandi Maja
       Man O Mandi Maja
       Man O Mandi Maja
       Wa Weshke Shee
       Nee Do Dem Ha

Arrive front. PAU-PUK-KEEWIS *rolls off poles, takes off Beaver head.*

PAU-PUK-KEEWIS:
    But the soul of Pau-Puk-Keewis
    Taking on a human shape —
    Northward fled into the forest.

COMPANY *attempt to stop him running U.S. with poles.* PAU-PUK-KEEWIS *escapes.* THE STORY-TELLER *threads his way through poles to front.*

STORY-TELLER:
    North he fled through the forest
    Crossed the wide and rushing rivers
    Past the mountains of the prairies
    To a lake with many islands
    Came the breathless Pau-Puk-Keewis
    Where among the water lilies
    Puhehuk the swan was sailing.

PAU-PUK-KEEWIS *dons swan's mask on fork lift truck. Goes up in the air.*

PAU-PUK-KEEWIS:
    Straightway changed into a swan,
    High above the ground he flew,

STORY-TELLER:
    High above the river forest,
    High above the Indian village
    Pau-Puk-Keewis flew in triumph.

All watch.

HIAWATHA:
Knew the voice of Hiawatha —

IAGOO:
Knew the outcry of Iagoo —

STORY-TELLER:
Hiawatha cried to heaven,
Waywassimo.

HIAWATHA:
Called Waywassimo, the lightning,

Lightning.

STORY-TELLER:
Annemeekee,

HIAWATHA:
And the thunder, Annemeekee

Thunder and wind.

STORY-TELLER:
And they came with night and darkness,
(*L.X. change*)
Sweeping down the Big Sea Water,
And the wind that blew behind him
Caught his mighty fan of feathers;
Sent him wheeling, whirling downward.

PAU-PUK-KEEWIS *dives into the outstretched arms of the* COMPANY *with drums and wind reaching climax.* THE COMPANY *lay him on the ground and stand looking at him.*

Dead among the village hunters,
Lay the cunning Pau-Puk-Keewis —
Lay the handsome mischief maker.
Ended were his wild adventures,

Ended were his tricks and gambols,
Ended all his craft and cunning,
Ended all his mischief making,
All his gambling and dancing,
All his wooing of the maidens.

*Take off his swan's head and wings. Replace with
eagle's head.*

HIAWATHA:
O Pau-Puk-Keewis!
Never more in human figure
Shall you search for new adventures,
Never more with jest and laughter
Dance the dust and leaves in whirlwinds,

Lift him upright, into the air.

But above there in the heavens
You shall soar and sail in circles;
I will change you to an eagle,
To Keneu, the great War Eagle.

Drums. PAU-PUK-KEEWIS *stands on* HIAWATHA'S
shoulders and is paraded slowly round.

STORY-TELLER:
And the name of Pau-Puk-Keewis
Lingers still among the people,
Lingers still among the singers,
And among the story-tellers;
And in Winter, when the snowflakes
Whirl in eddies round the lodges,

COMPANY *wave white fur cloaks. L.X. change.*

When the wind in gusty tumult
O'er the smoke-flues pipes and whistles,

ONE:
'There', they cry, 'comes Pau-Puk-Keewis'

   He is dancing through the village,

   He is gathering in his harvest!

L.X. Snow. Flute. COMPANY *wrap white fur cloaks round them and move slowly in circle.*

THE FAMINE

STORY-TELLER:
   O the long and dreary winter!
   O the cold and cruel winter!

One by one COMPANY *lay white cloaks on cross-poles of tipi lying on ground.*

   Ever thicker, thicker, thicker,
   Froze the ice on lake and river,
   Ever deeper, deeper, deeper
   Fell the snow o'er all the landscape,
   Fell the covering snow and drifted
   Through the forest, round the village.

CHIBIABOS *and* KWASIND *don black blankets and pass* THE STORY-TELLER.

   Gone was gentle Chibiabos,
   Gone the gentle strong-man Kwasind,
   To the islands of the Blessed,
   To the land of ghosts and shadows.

MINNEHAHA *lies in centre.*

   All the earth was sick and famished,
   Hungry was the air around them,
   Hungry was the sky above them,
   And the hungry stars in heaven
   Like the eyes of wolves glared at them!

Red pin-spots of light appear in the gloom. HIA-
WATHA *kneels by* MINNEHAHA. *Strange sounds.*

> Came two guests, of gloom and silence
> Looked with haggard eyes and hollow
> At the face of Laughing Water.

FEVER *and* FAMINE *in black cloaks and masks.*

FAMINE:
> Behold me!
> I am Famine, Bukadawin!

FEVER:
> Behold me!
> I am Fever, Ahkosewin!

NOKOMIS *kneels by her.*

STORY-TELLER:
> And the lovely Minnehaha
> Shuddered as they looked upon her,
> Lay there, trembling, freezing, burning.

HIAWATHA *goes up on fork-lift.*

> Forth into the empty forest,
> Rushed the maddened Hiawatha.

HIAWATHA:
> Gitche Manito, the Mighty!
> Give us food, or we must perish!
> Give me food for Minnehaha,
> For my dying Minnehaha!

FEVER *and* FAMINE *beckon.*

STORY-TELLER:
> But there came no other answer
> Than the echo of the woodlands,

CHORUS (*whispered*):
> Minnehaha! Minnehaha!

MINNEHAHA:
> Hark! I hear a rushing,
> Hear a roaring and a rushing,
> Hear the Falls of Minnehaha
> Calling to me from a distance.

NOKOMIS:
> No, my child,
> 'Tis the night-wind in the pine trees!

MINNEHAHA:
> Look! I see my father
> Standing lonely at his doorway,
> Beckoning to me from his wigwam,
> In the land of the Dacotahs!

THE STORY-TELLER *comes slowly from back with long white pole.*

NOKOMIS:
> No, my child!
> 'Tis the smoke that waves and beckons!

MINNEHAHA:
> Ah! the eyes of Pauguk
> Glare upon me in the darkness;
> I can feel his icy fingers
> Clasping mine amid the darkness!

MINNEHAHA *grasps white pole which gradually slips from her fingers.* MINNEHAHA *falls back.*

CHORUS (*whispered*):
> Hiawatha! Hiawatha!

STORY-TELLER:
> And the desolate Hiawatha,
> Far away amid the forest,
> Heard the voice of Minnehaha.

CHORUS (*whispered*):
    Hiawatha! Hiawatha!

STORY-TELLER:
    And he rushed into the wigwam,
    Saw his lovely Minnehaha
    Lying dead and cold before him;
    Uttered such a cry of anguish,
    That the very stars in heaven
    Shook and trembled with his anguish.

All wrap white fur round MINNEHAHA.

NOKOMIS:
    Then they buried Minnehaha;
    In the snow a grave they made her,
    Covered her with snow, like ermine,
    Thus they buried Minnehaha.

COMPANY *lift her in the air on the cross-poles.*
Fire F.X.

STORY-TELLER:
    And at night a fire was lighted,
    On her grave four times was kindled,
    For her soul upon its journey
    To the islands of the Blessed.

The COMPANY *parade round holding* MINNEHAHA
high in the air.

BURIAL SONG

ALL: He He-A-Wana, Wa-Wa-Te
                    He He-A-Wana, Wa-Wa-Te
                    Wasna, Wa-Ha Tin Te
                    Wasna, Wa-Ha Tin Te.
                    (*3 times*)

During second and third verses MINNEHAHA *is*

60

lowered, unwrapped and the furs and poles struck.
End of sequence, drum roll and L.X. change.
COMPANY *sit in semi-circle.* IAGOO *circles stage*
and comes centre.

THE WHITE MAN'S FOOT

STORY-TELLER:
From his wanderings far to eastward,
From the regions of the morning,
Homeward now returned Iagoo,
The greater traveller, the greater boaster,
Full of new and strange adventures.

IAGOO:
I have seen a water
Bigger than the Big Sea-Water,
Broader than the Gitche Gumee,
Bitter so that none could drink it!

ALL:
It cannot be so!
It cannot be so!

IAGOO:
O'er it, o'er this water
Came a great canoe with pinions,
A canoe with wings came flying,
Bigger than a grove of pine-trees
Taller than the tallest tree-tops!

ALL:
We don't believe it!
We don't believe it!

IAGOO:
From its mouth to greet him
Came Waywassimo, the lightning,
Came the thunder, Annemeekee!

ALL:
>   What tales you tell us!

IAGOO:
>   In it, came a people,
>   In the great canoe with pinions
>   Came a hundred warriors,
>   Painted white were all their faces,
>   And with hair their chins were covered.

ALL:
>   What lies you tell us!
>   Do not think that we believe them!

STORY-TELLER:
>   Only Hiawatha laughed not,
>   But he gravely spake and answered
>   To their jeering and their jesting:

> HIAWATHA *stands with* IAGOO.

HIAWATHA:
>   True is all Iagoo tells us;

> *Shadow of* CAVALRY OFFICER *appears on disc.*
> *Faint sound of a military march on a snare drum.*

>   I have seen it in a vision,
>   Seen the great canoe with pinions,
>   Seen the people with white faces,
>   Seen the coming of this bearded
>   People of the wooden vessel
>   From the regions of the morning,
>   From the shining land of Wabun.
>   Gitche Manito the Mighty
>   Sends them to us with his message.
>   Let us welcome then the strangers,
>   Hail them as our friends and brothers.

> *Shadow fades.*

I beheld, too, in that vision,
All the secrets of the future,
All the land was full of people,
Restless, struggling, toiling, striving,
In the woodlands rang their axes,
Smoked their towns in all the valleys,
Over all the lakes and rivers,
Rushed their great canoes of thunder.

CAVALRY OFFICER *appears on fork-lift truck in
front of disc.*

I beheld our nations scattered,
Weakened, warring with each other,
Saw the remnants of our people
Sweeping westward, wild and woeful,
Like the cloud-rack of a tempest,
Like the withered leaves of Autumn!

Drum builds to climax. The CAVALRY OFFICER
*turns to audience and fires live revolver shot followed
by thunder. Flute follows.* HIAWATHA *stands D.S.
in front of two crossed poles from tipi frame.* COM-
PANY *stand behind him.*

HIAWATHA'S DEPARTURE

STORY-TELLER:
By the shore of Gitche Gumee,
By the shining Big Sea Water,
At the doorway of his wigwam,
In the pleasant summer morning,
Hiawatha stood and waited.
Stood and waited for death to take him.
Toward the sun his hands were lifted,
Both the palms spread out against it,
And between the parted fingers
Fell the sunshine on his features.

HIAWATHA:

    I am going, O my people,
    On a long and distant journey;
    Many moons and many winters
    Will have come, and will have vanished,
    Ere I come again and see you.
    White man's foot I leave behind me;
    Listen to the words of wisdom,
    Listen to the truth they tell you,
    For the Master of Life has sent them,
    From the land of light and morning.

COMPANY *bring canoe from back.*

STORY-TELLER:

    On the shore stood Hiawatha,
    Turned and waved his hand at parting;
    On the clear and luminous water
    Launched his birch canoe for sailing,

HIAWATHA *gets in canoe.*

    Whispered to it: 'Westward! Westward!'
    And with speed it darted forward.

COMPANY *lift canoe in air and move to place it on fork-lift truck.* THE STORY-TELLER *kneels front.*

    And the evening sun descending
    Set the clouds on fire with redness,
    Burned a broad sky, like a prairie,
    Left upon the level water
    One long track and trail of splendour,

COMPANY *turned with hands in air facing U.S.* HIAWATHA *goes up in air in front of disc, silhouetted in sunset. Wind softly.*

    Down whose stream, as down a river,
    Westward, westward Hiawatha

Sailed into the fiery sunset,
Sailed into the purple vapours,
Sailed into the dusk of evening.

Thus departed Hiawatha,
Hiawatha the Beloved,
In the glory of the sunset,
In the purple mists of evening,
To the regions of the home-wind,
Of the North West wind, Keewaydin,
To the islands of the Blessed,
To the land of the Hereafter!

Drums. COMPANY *get drums and stomp round to
opening chorus.*

Yo yo wi ha (*once*)

The COMPANY *stomp off, the sound gradually dying.*

THE END